Amina's Ramadan Journey

Anila Asif

Published by Anila Asif, 2024.

AMINA 'S RAMADAN JOURNEY

First edition. December 26, 2024.

ISBN: 979-8230293897

Written by Anila Asif.

Amina's Ramadan Journey

Chapter 1:
The Excitement Begins

It was the start of a very special month in the town of Sunnyville. The sun was shining brightly, but there was a sense of excitement in the air. The air felt different today—so full of promise. It was the first day of Ramadan, and the children of the town could feel it!

In a cozy little house at the end of Willow Lane, a young girl named Amina woke up early.

She could hear the soft chirping of birds outside and the gentle rustling of leaves in the breeze. As she rubbed her eyes and stretched, she remembered the special day that was about to begin. The night before, her parents had been talking about Ramadan—the sacred month when Muslims fast from sunrise to sunset. They had explained to Amina how this month helps everyone grow closer to Allah and teaches them to be kind, patient, and grateful.

It was the first time Amina would experience Ramadan, and she was full of excitement.
"Good morning, Amina! Are you ready to start our Ramadan journey?" her mom asked with a warm smile, as she entered Amina's room holding a tray with a cup of warm tea.
Amina jumped out of bed with wide eyes. "Yes, Mama! I'm so excited! I want to learn all about it!"
Her mom chuckled, setting the tray down on the table.
"Ramadan is a very special month for Muslims.

It's a time to think about others and help those in need. We fast from sunrise to sunset, which means we don't eat or drink during the day. But Ramadan is not just about fasting; it's about becoming a better person. It teaches us to be patient, kind, and grateful for everything we have."

Amina listened closely, trying to understand all the new things her mom was teaching her. "So, we don't eat all day?"

"That's right, sweetie," her mom said gently. "But we break our fast at sunset with a special meal called iftar. That's the time when families come together, share food, and feel thankful for all the blessings in their lives."

Amina's eyes sparkled. "I can't wait for my first iftar, Mama! Will there be lots of food?"

Her mom smiled warmly. "Yes, we'll have dates, fruits, water, and all kinds of delicious foods to share with our family."

Amina had heard about the delicious foods at iftar from her friends at school. Her tummy rumbled just thinking about it, but she understood why fasting was important. She knew it wasn't just about waiting for food—it was about learning patience, feeling empathy for others who don't have enough to eat, and showing kindness to everyone around her.

As she looked out the window, the morning sky was filled with soft colors of pink and gold.

The sun was just beginning to rise, and Amina felt a sense of calm. Today marked the beginning of something beautiful. It wasn't just the start of a month—it was the beginning of a journey that would teach her how to be more thoughtful, caring, and thankful.

"I think I'm going to like Ramadan, Mama," Amina said, her heart full of happiness. Her mom hugged her tightly.

"I know you will, my dear. It's a month filled with blessings, love, and joy. And we'll experience it together, as a family."

Amina smiled and nodded, ready for the adventure that lay ahead. She couldn't wait to learn everything about Ramadan and be part of something so special.

The day had just begun, and Amina knew this Ramadan would be one she would never forget.

Chapter 2:
Fasting Like the Grown-Ups

The next day, Amina woke up early, long before the sun rose. She heard the soft sounds of birds chirping outside and saw the first light of dawn creeping through the curtains. The house was quiet, but there was a sense of excitement in the air. Today, Amina would experience her first day of fasting during Ramadan, just like the grown-ups.

Amina joined her family at the dining table for a special breakfast called "Suhoor." This was the meal they ate before the sun came up, to prepare them for the long day ahead. Her father smiled at her as she sat down with her small bowl of porridge. "This is an important meal, Amina," he said. "It helps give us the energy we need for the day, especially since we won’t be eating until sunset.

But remember, Ramadan is about more than just not eating. It's about becoming a better person, showing kindness, and helping others." Amina nodded, thinking deeply about her father's words. "I understand, Papa," she said with a bright smile. "I'll be kind today and try to help Mama with the house." She wanted to make her parents proud, and helping others felt like the right thing to do.

After Suhoor, Amina got ready for the day. She put on her favorite dress and spent some time playing with her little brother, Sami. But as the hours passed, she started to feel a little hungry. The clock on the wall seemed to tick more slowly than ever.

She watched as her parents went about their day, busy with work and chores. Amina tried to focus on her games, but her stomach growled softly, reminding her that she hadn’t eaten anything since the early morning.

"It's okay," Amina whispered to herself. "I can do this. I just need to stay patient."

She remembered what her mom and dad had taught her—fasting wasn't just about staying away from food and drink; it was about learning to be patient and to feel empathy for others. People who don't have enough to eat experience hunger every day, and Ramadan helps remind everyone to be thankful for what they have and to share with those in need.

The hours dragged on, and Amina felt her energy starting to dip. But she kept herself busy by helping her mom in the kitchen, cleaning up the toys she and Sami had played with, and even setting the table for iftar. The thought of the delicious food they would share later gave her strength. As the sun began to set, Amina could feel a sense of anticipation in the air. She knew the moment was coming soon—the moment when she would break her fast.

She could already smell the wonderful scent of food cooking in the kitchen, and her heart skipped a beat.
At last, the call to prayer echoed through the town, signaling that it was time to break the fast. Amina's family gathered together at the table. With a smile on her face, Amina reached for a date and a glass of water, as her father had taught her. "Bismillah," she said, which means "In the name of Allah," before taking a bite.

The sweet taste of the date was like a little burst of joy. She could feel the energy returning to her body.

“Alhamdulillah,” Amina said softly, meaning "Praise be to God." She felt a warm sense of pride fill her heart. It had been tough, but she had done it. She had fasted all day, just like the grown-ups, and it made her feel stronger and closer to Allah.

After the dates and water, the family enjoyed a delicious meal together.

The table was filled with colorful dishes—fluffy rice, roasted chicken, crispy samosas, and fresh salad. Amina felt so grateful for the food in front of her, and even more thankful for the lessons Ramadan was teaching her. “Papa, I did it!” Amina exclaimed between bites, her eyes shining. “I stayed patient all day, just like you said.”

Her father smiled warmly and patted her on the back. "I'm proud of you, Amina. You've learned something important today. Ramadan is not easy, but it makes us stronger and helps us become better people. You did a wonderful job."

Amina smiled, feeling proud of herself. It wasn't easy, but she had learned so much already. And she couldn't wait to continue her Ramadan journey with her family.

Chapter 3:
Helping Hands

One sunny afternoon, Amina and her best friend, Omar, were outside playing in the yard. They ran around, giggling and enjoying the warm breeze that danced through the trees. They played tag, pretending to be superheroes, and chased each other around the garden, laughing all the way.

But suddenly, in the middle of their fun, Amina stopped and looked thoughtful.

Something had just come to her mind, something important she had been thinking about since the beginning of Ramadan. She looked at Omar, her eyes sparkling with excitement.

“Omar, we should help others during Ramadan!” Amina said, her voice filled with enthusiasm.

Omar paused, his face brightening as he stopped running. “That’s a great idea, Amina! But how can we help?”

Amina thought for a moment, her fingers tapping her chin.

. “We can give food to people who don’t have enough. We could collect some things and take them to the mosque where they’re gathering donations for those in need!” Omar nodded eagerly. “Yes! Let’s do it! We can fill a box with food and help make someone’s Ramadan better!” The two friends rushed inside, excited to begin their mission. Amina’s mom helped them gather food from the kitchen. They packed rice, bread, fruits, and other goodies into a big cardboard box.

Amina also added some homemade cookies she had baked with her mom the day before, thinking that a sweet treat would bring a smile to someone's face.

Once the box was packed, Amina and Omar grabbed it together, each holding one side of the heavy box. They walked to the local mosque, their hearts filled with excitement and joy. The mosque was a place where people came to pray and also to give to those in need. Amina knew it was the perfect place to help.

When they arrived at the mosque, they were greeted by a kind lady who was in charge of the food drive. She smiled warmly at the children, noticing the box they carried. “Hello, children! How wonderful to see you here. What do you have for us today?” she asked, her voice full of kindness.
“We brought this box of food,” Amina said proudly. “We wanted to help people who might not have enough to eat.”

The lady's face lit up. "You both are doing a wonderful thing," she said with a smile. "Your generosity will make someone's Ramadan a little brighter. Thank you so much!" Amina and Omar felt a warm, happy feeling in their hearts. It was such a good feeling to know that their small act of kindness would make a big difference in someone's life. Amina realized that helping others was one of the most beautiful parts of Ramadan.

It made her feel closer to the true spirit of the month—giving, caring, and being thankful for what she had. As they left the mosque, Amina and Omar walked side by side, their hearts filled with joy. The afternoon sun seemed to shine even brighter, and the world felt full of possibilities. Amina knew that Ramadan was teaching her so much about being a kind and generous person. It wasn't just about fasting; it was about showing love and care for everyone around her.

"I'm so happy we did that, Omar," Amina said, smiling at her friend.

"Me too, Amina!" Omar replied. "I think we should do this every year!"

Amina's heart swelled with pride as they walked home together. She had learned an important lesson today: true happiness comes from helping others. And with Ramadan still in full swing, she couldn't wait to think of more ways to give and share kindness with those around her.

Chapter 4:
The Spirit of Kindnes

As the days of Ramadan passed by, Amina couldn't help but think about how she could be kinder to everyone around her. Every day, she tried to show more love and care for her family, her friends, and even the people she didn't know very well. She remembered her parents' words about the true spirit of Ramadan: it wasn't just about fasting or giving to charity, but about becoming a better person—patient, kind, and respectful.

One afternoon, as Amina was sitting on the couch reading a book, she heard a loud crash in the kitchen. She jumped up and rushed to see what had happened. To her surprise, she found her little brother, Sami, standing near the kitchen table with a look of worry on his face. There was juice spilled all over the carpet, and the glass was shattered on the floor.

“Oh no!” Sami exclaimed, his eyes wide with panic. “I didn’t mean to! I’m sorry, Amina!”

Amina could have gotten upset. After all, the juice had spilled all over the new carpet, and it was going to take a lot of cleaning. But instead of feeling frustrated, Amina took a deep breath and smiled.

"It's okay, Sami," Amina said gently, walking over to him. "Don't worry! We can clean it together."

Sami's eyes brightened a little, relieved by his sister's kind words. "Really? You're not mad at me?"

Amina shook her head. "No, I'm not mad. Accidents happen, and it's okay.

Let's clean it up together, and we'll make it all better." Amina grabbed a towel from the counter, and Sami helped by picking up the broken pieces of the glass. Together, they wiped the juice from the carpet, and soon the kitchen was looking as good as new. Amina's heart felt light and happy, knowing she had helped Sami without getting upset. She had been patient, just like her parents had taught her.

Later that evening, as the family gathered around the dinner table to break their fast, Amina's parents noticed how she had been extra kind to Sami all day. They were both proud of her.

"You know, Amina," her mom said, smiling warmly, "today you really showed the spirit of Ramadan. Instead of getting upset, you were kind and patient with your brother. That's exactly what Ramadan is all about."

Amina felt a warm feeling in her heart. “Thank you, Mama,” she said shyly, but with a big smile.

Her dad added, “During Ramadan, it’s not just about fasting and giving to others. It’s about showing kindness, respect, and patience in everything we do. You’re doing a wonderful job, Amina. Keep it up!”

Amina beamed with pride. She had always thought that fasting was the most important part of Ramadan, but now she realized that being kind to others was just as important.

She remembered all the little things her parents had taught her about the spirit of Ramadan—helping others, being patient, and treating everyone with respect.

That evening, after dinner, Amina lay in bed thinking about her day. She felt happy and peaceful, knowing that kindness was something she could practice every day, not just during Ramadan. She realized that even small acts of kindness could make the world a better place.

"I'm going to try to be even kinder tomorrow," Amina whispered to herself before drifting off to sleep. She was excited for the days ahead, knowing that every act of kindness brought her closer to the true meaning of Ramadan. And as the moon shone brightly outside her window, Amina smiled, grateful for all the lessons she had learned and excited for the many more to come.

Chapter 5:
The Night of Power

One warm evening, as the stars twinkled in the dark sky like tiny diamonds, Amina sat with her family in the living room. They had just finished their Iftar and were now relaxing together. The air was filled with a peaceful, quiet energy, and Amina could feel that something special was about to happen.

Her parents had been talking about the last ten days of Ramadan, and tonight was one of the most important nights of all.

"Amina," her dad began softly, "I want to tell you about something very special that happens during the last ten nights of Ramadan. It's called Laylat al-Qadr, the Night of Power."

Amina's eyes widened with curiosity. She had never heard of it before.

"What is Laylat al-Qadr, Papa?" she asked, her voice filled with excitement.

Her father smiled and explained, “Laylat al-Qadr is the night when the Quran was first revealed to the Prophet Muhammad (peace be upon him). It’s the most blessed night of Ramadan, and it is said that on this night, Allah listens to all our prayers and grants us special blessings.”

Amina’s heart fluttered at the thought. "So, this night is extra special? Allah will hear our prayers and give us blessings?"

“Yes,” her father replied gently.

"It's a night full of mercy and grace. During this night, our good deeds are multiplied, and Allah is closer to us than ever. It's a time to pray, make du'a (supplication), and ask for all the good things we want—both for ourselves and for others."

Amina felt a deep sense of excitement. She wanted to make the most of this special night, to be close to Allah and pray for the things that mattered most.

It was the perfect opportunity to ask for blessings—not just for herself, but for everyone she loved and even for people she didn't know.

That night, Amina stayed up late with her family. The house was quiet except for the soft sound of their voices as they prayed together. Amina felt a peaceful calm in her heart as she made du'a, asking Allah for blessings for her family, her friends, and all the people in the world.

She prayed for the health and happiness of everyone she loved, for the safety of people who were struggling, and for peace and kindness to fill the world. Each prayer felt so important, and Amina could feel the warmth of the night wrapping around her, as if her prayers were being heard and answered.

After a while, Amina closed her eyes and whispered a quiet prayer of her own: “I hope Allah blesses everyone around the world, especially those who are suffering.

Please make the world a better place for everyone."

Her heart felt full of gratitude as she lay in bed that night, the stars still shining brightly outside her window. Amina felt peaceful, knowing that she had made the most of Laylat al-Qadr by praying with all her heart. The quiet of the night felt so comforting, like a soft blanket wrapping around her, making her feel safe and loved.

As she drifted off to sleep, Amina's mind replayed all the prayers she had made and all the blessings she had asked for.

She felt content and happy, knowing that Laylat al-Qadr was a night full of mercy and blessings, and she had been a part of it.

"Alhamdulillah," Amina whispered softly as she closed her eyes, drifting into a peaceful sleep, grateful for the chance to connect with Allah on such a special night.

And as she slept, she knew in her heart that her prayers would be heard, and the blessings of the Night of Power would bring peace, love, and kindness to the world.

Chapter 6:
Eid Celebration

After a month of fasting, helping others, and being kind, Ramadan was coming to an end. The entire town of Sunnyville seemed to buzz with excitement. The air was filled with joy and anticipation because tomorrow would be Eid—the special day marking the end of Ramadan. It was a day of celebration, togetherness, and gratitude.

On the morning of Eid, Amina woke up early, her heart full of excitement. The sun had just risen, and the house was filled with the sweet scent of freshly brewed tea and baking treats. It was the first Eid that Amina could truly understand and appreciate, and she couldn't wait for the celebrations to begin.

"Good morning, Amina! Eid Mubarak!" her mom said as she hugged her tightly. "Today is the day to celebrate all the good things we've done during Ramadan."

Amina smiled brightly and replied, “Eid Mubarak, Mama! Thank you for teaching me so much this month. I’ve learned so much about kindness, helping others, and being patient.”

Her parents had a special surprise for her. Her mom handed her a beautifully wrapped gift. Amina’s eyes sparkled as she eagerly unwrapped it. Inside, she found a lovely new dress, perfect for Eid.

"Thank you, Mama! It's so beautiful!" Amina exclaimed, her face lighting up with joy.

Her mom smiled. "It's a gift to celebrate all the wonderful things you've done this Ramadan. You've grown so much, Amina."

Amina quickly changed into her new dress, feeling so proud and happy. She was ready to join in the festivities, not just for the presents, but because she knew that Eid was a day of thanking Allah for all the blessings in her life.

Once they were all dressed and ready, Amina and her family made their way to the mosque. The streets were filled with people in their finest clothes, greeting each other with “Eid Mubarak!” It was a beautiful sight—everyone, young and old, smiling and sharing the joy of this blessed day.

When they arrived at the mosque, it was filled with the sounds of laughter and greetings.

Eid Mubarak!

Amina could feel the warmth of the community around her. The mosque was decorated with colorful lights and flowers, and the air was filled with excitement and gratitude. People gathered in rows to offer the special Eid prayer. Amina stood beside her parents as they prayed together. It felt so peaceful and special. After the prayer, everyone greeted one another with hugs and cheerful "Eid Mubarak" wishes.

Amina felt so thankful. She had spent the entire month learning about Ramadan and growing closer to Allah, but today—on Eid—she felt the full happiness and reward of everything she had done. The whole community was united in joy, and Amina knew that it was a day of blessings for everyone.

After the prayer, they went to visit their neighbors, exchanging food and gifts.

Amina's family brought homemade sweets, and their neighbors gave them delicious food in return. There was laughter, love, and kindness everywhere. Amina loved seeing everyone so happy and grateful, and she felt a deep sense of connection to everyone around her.

As the day went on, Amina spent time with her friends and family. They played games, shared stories, and enjoyed delicious meals together.

The best part was knowing that this celebration wasn't just about fun—it was about appreciating the blessings of Ramadan and remembering all the good deeds they had done throughout the month. When the sun began to set, Amina sat with her family, feeling content and grateful. She looked around at the smiling faces of her parents, little brother Sami, and all their friends and neighbors.

The whole day had been filled with love, laughter, and gratitude, and Amina felt so blessed to have experienced it all.

“Eid Mubarak, everyone!” Amina cheered, her heart full of love and joy. “This has been the best day ever!”

As the evening drew to a close, Amina reflected on her first Ramadan. It had been a month of fasting, prayer, kindness, and giving. She had learned so many important lessons, not just about her faith, but about the importance of family, community, and helping those in need.

Ramadan had made her a better person, and she knew she would carry these lessons with her all year long.
As she lay in bed that night, feeling peaceful and content, Amina whispered to herself, “Insha’Allah, next year I’ll be even better. I’ll do more good deeds and help more people.”
With a smile on her face and love in her heart, Amina drifted off to sleep,

looking forward to the next Ramadan, knowing it would bring even more blessings, love, and happiness.

And so, Amina's first Ramadan came to an end, leaving her with beautiful memories and valuable lessons that would last a lifetime—lessons of kindness, generosity, patience, and gratitude that she would carry with her always.

"Eid Mubarak, everyone!" Amina said one last time, her heart overflowing with joy and gratitude for the amazing month she had experienced.

www.ingramcontent.com/pod-product-compliance
Lightning Source LLC
LaVergne TN
LVHW090125160826
845673LV00015B/1024